JEAN CRAIGHEAD GEORGE

The EAGLES *Are* BACK

PAINTINGS BY WENDELL MINOR

Dial Books for Young Readers · An imprint of Penguin Group (USA) Inc.

ACKNOWLEDGMENTS

The artist would like to thank his photographer friends and colleagues: Thomas Mangelsen and Robert Shaw, who gave me access to their photographs of eagles as reference for my paintings in this book; and special thanks to Charlie Craighead, who supplied images of eagles' nests and was my guide in Yellowstone, where we viewed bald eagles in flight and visited a nesting site. Last, but not least, great thanks to Jean Craighead George for bringing to light, in this third book of a series, environmental success stories that show us it is possible to preserve nature for future generations. — Wendell Minor

A list of websites to consult about bald eagles is included on page 32.

DIAL BOOKS FOR YOUNG READERS · A division of Penguin Young Readers Group · Published by the Penguin Group
Penguin Group (USA) Inc., 375 Hudson Street, New York, New York 10014, U.S.A. · Penguin Group (Canada), 90 Eglinton Avenue East, Suite 700, Toronto, Ontario, Canada M4P 2Y3 (a division of Pearson Penguin Canada Inc.) · Penguin Books Ltd, 80 Strand, London WC2R 0RL, England · Penguin Ireland, 25 St Stephen's Green, Dublin 2, Ireland (a division of Penguin Books Ltd) · Penguin Group (Australia), 250 Camberwell Road, Camberwell, Victoria 3124, Australia (a division of Pearson Australia Group Pty Ltd) · Penguin Books India Pvt Ltd, 11 Community Centre, Panchsheel Park, New Delhi - 110 017, India · Penguin Group (NZ), 67 Apollo Drive, Rosedale, Auckland 0632, New Zealand (a division of Pearson New Zealand Ltd) · Penguin Books (South Africa) (Pty) Ltd, 24 Sturdee Avenue, Rosebank, Johannesburg 2196, South Africa
Penguin Books Ltd, Registered Offices: 80 Strand, London WC2R 0RL, England

The art was created using Winsor & Newton designer's guoache and watercolor with pencil on Strathmore 500 bristol board.

Library of Congress Cataloging-in-Publication Data
George, Jean Craighead, date.
The eagles are back / Jean Craighead George ; paintings by Wendell Minor. p.   cm.
Includes bibliographical references. ISBN 978-0-8037-3771-6 (hardcover) 1. Bald eagle—Juvenile literature. 2. Endangered species—Juvenile literature.
I. Minor, Wendell. II. Title. QL696.F32G455 2013   598.9'42—dc23   2012005717

To Barbara Dana, who soars high

JEAN CRAIGHEAD GEORGE

To all those who have helped
save our national symbol

WENDELL MINOR

Years ago a boy climbed to an eagle nest in an old tree by a remote lake. The nest belonged to a pair of bald eagles he had named Uncle Sam and First Lady. He had not seen them here for a while.

His friend, the ranger, had said the bald eagles were vanishing from the earth, and he was worried.

The boy reached the aerie, a six-foot platform of sticks and limbs that was the eagles' nest. Two smashed eggs lay at his feet.

The boy knew that the majestic bald eagle was the national bird of the United States. The Founding Fathers chose the eagle because of its power and beauty. There were half a million bald eagles when the Puritans landed.

There was another reason bald eagles were the national bird. They help the little creatures. With their strong beaks they tear open the leather-skinned salmon and the other game that the foxes and crows cannot. They eat some, fly away, and a cycle begins. The crows drop bits of food, and the turtles get it. The turtles drop pieces to the salamanders, who drop bits to the crayfish, who scatter the food to the fairy shrimp and tiny copepods. A nation of small animal citizens is sustained by the magnificent bald eagle.

Bald eagles were now scarce in the United States. They were down to about 450 pairs when the boy picked up the eggshells and climbed down the tree.

Why? Cities had taken over land where eagles soared. Hunters had slaughtered them. But mainly the pesticide DDT had done them in. It came up the food chain from the copepods to the insects to the fish to the fish-eating eagles. The DDT softened their eggs' shells so that they broke when the eagles sat on the eggs to incubate them. Bird lovers discovered that the eagles were becoming scarce and scientists discovered the deadly effects of DDT. Congress banned its use.

The boy was sad because he had watched Uncle Sam and First Lady raise eaglets every year for as long as he could remember. The shore and woods had danced with the humble wildlife that were fed by the mighty eagles.

Now all were eerily silent.

Suddenly Uncle Sam plummeted from one thousand feet above and caught a fish.

"There you are," the boy cheered. "Hooray, you old sharp eyes, you're back."

The boy was on his way home when he met his friend, the ranger. The ranger showed him a precious eagle egg he was carrying. A ranger in Alaska had sent it to him. It was part of a many-faceted campaign to save the eagle.

"This is the only pair I know about," the ranger said. "So I'm hoping Uncle Sam and First Lady will adopt this egg. Sometimes eagles do. But I can't watch this pair because I have to go to another park for a while."

"I can watch," the boy said. "Uncle Sam and First Lady are my friends. Once we caught fish together."

"Things are changing for the better for the eagles," the ranger said. "It is illegal to shoot them. DDT has been banned by Congress. Scientists are trying every trick they know to bring the eagle back. I am trying with this egg. I hope Uncle Sam and First Lady will help me."

"So do I," said the boy.

The ranger thanked the boy for volunteering to watch the nest for him and climbed up the old tree. High on the aerie he placed the egg in the stick-filled nest.

"Good luck, Egg," he said, and returned to the boy.

"If Uncle Sam and First Lady do not come back in four days," he said, "your duties are over. They will never be back."

The next day at dawn the boy ran back to the old tree. He whistled for the eagles. They did not answer.

The boy returned the second day and whistled for the regal birds.

They did not appear.

On the third day the boy called their names from dawn to dusk. They did not answer.

The setting sun had reached the horizon and the trees were bending in the wind when suddenly out of sky came Uncle Sam and First Lady. They alighted on the nest and stared at the egg.

"Please, please," called the boy, "sit down and incubate."

First Lady cried softly. She shook out her feathers and lifted them as if to brood the egg. Then she flew away.

Uncle Sam called to her, but she disappeared in the clouds. He walked to the egg and looked at it. The sun disappeared. The wind blew cold. Uncle Sam ruffled his feathers and sat down on the egg.

Just before darkness First Lady returned. Uncle Sam lifted his six-foot wings and was airborne. First Lady sat down in his place. They had adopted the egg.

The boy went home whistling and grinning. "I will tell the ranger," he said.

Twenty-eight days later the egg from Alaska hatched. The eaglet was wobbly and thin. The boy avidly caught fish and threw them to Uncle Sam and First Lady. They snagged them in their talons and fed them to their adopted daughter, Alaska.

Alaska the eaglet grew.

She learned to stand up and flap her wings.

One day the ranger returned. He cheered to see the eaglet.

"Alaska is ready to fly," said the boy.

"Not yet," said the ranger. "The books say she's not quite ready."

Then a wind gusted under Alaska's wings and lifted her off the aerie.

She flapped her wings—and *was* flying!

Uncle Sam and First Lady dropped out of the sky and flew with her.
Three bald eagles soared in the thermal winds.

Many years later a man and his son were walking a trail high above the Hudson River.
The man looked down on the waterway and shouted. "Johnny, the eagles are back!"
He grinned as he pointed to about 30 bald eagles around them. They were soaring over
the water, the boats, the river shores, and the trees.

"That's neat," said his son. "I read all about the return of the eagles on the Internet.

"And you know what?" he said. "A boy about my age is supposed to have helped bring the eagles back from extinction.

"That boy caught fish and tossed them to a pair of eagles who fed them to their adopted eaglet and raised her to adulthood. Great legend."

"That is not a legend" said the man. "I am that boy."

The eagles are back.

SOURCES

Selected websites for more information about bald eagles:

http://baldeagles.org/preserve

http://www.npca.org/wildlife_protection/wildlife_facts/baldeagle.html

http://www.sandiegozoo.org/animalbytes/t-bald_eagle.html

http://nationalzoo.si.edu/animals/northamerica/baldeaglerefuge/eaglefacts.cfm

http://www.nwf.org/News-and-Magazines/National-Wildlife/Birds/Archives/2010/Seeing-bald-eagles.aspx